RUBBER RING

A Solo Play

by James McDermott

samuelfrench.co.uk

FOR AMATEUR PRODUCTION ENQUIRIES

UNITED KINGDOM AND WORLD
EXCLUDING NORTH AMERICA
plays@samuelfrench.co.uk
020 7255 4302/01

Each title is subject to availability from Samuel French,
depending upon country of performance.

THINKING ABOUT PERFORMING A SHOW?

There are thousands of plays and musicals available to perform from Samuel French right now, and applying for a licence is easier and more affordable than you might think

---

From classic plays to brand new musicals, from monologues to epic dramas, there are shows for everyone.

Plays and musicals are protected by copyright law, so if you want to perform them, the first thing you'll need is a licence. This simple process helps support the playwright by ensuring they get paid for their work and means that you'll have the documents you need to stage the show in public.

Not all our shows are available to perform all the time, so it's important to check and apply for a licence before you start rehearsals or commit to doing the show.

LEARN MORE & FIND THOUSANDS OF SHOWS

Browse our full range of plays and musicals, and find out more about how to license a show

www.samuelfrench.co.uk/perform

Talk to the friendly experts in our Licensing team for advice on choosing a show and help with licensing

plays@samuelfrench.co.uk   020 7387 9373

Acting Editions

BORN TO PERFORM

Playscripts designed from the ground up to work the way you do in rehearsal, performance and study

---

Larger, clearer text for easier reading

Wider margins for notes

Performance features such as character and props lists, sound and lighting cues, and more

---

+ CHOOSE A SIZE AND STYLE TO SUIT YOU

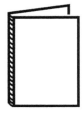

STANDARD EDITION

Our regular paperback book at our regular size

SPIRAL-BOUND EDITION

The same size as the Standard Edition, but with a sturdy, easy-to-fold, easy-to-hold spiral-bound spine

LARGE EDITION

A4 size and spiral bound, with larger text and a blank page for notes opposite every page of text – perfect for technical and directing use

---

LEARN MORE | **samuelfrench.co.uk/actingeditions**

MUSIC USE NOTE

Licensees are solely responsible for obtaining formal written permission from copyright owners to use copyrighted music in the performance of this play and are strongly cautioned to do so. If no such permission is obtained by the licensee, then the licensee must use only original music that the licensee owns and controls. Licensees are solely responsible and liable for all music clearances and shall indemnify the copyright owners of the play(s) and their licensing agent, Samuel French, against any costs, expenses, losses and liabilities arising from the use of music by licensees. Please contact the appropriate music licensing authority in your territory for the rights to any incidental music.

IMPORTANT BILLING AND CREDIT REQUIREMENTS

If you have obtained performance rights to this title, please refer to your licensing agreement for important billing and credit requirements.

ABOUT THE AUTHOR

James McDermott trained at the University of East Anglia where he graduated with an MA (Distinction) in Scriptwriting. He has participated in the Royal Court Writers' Group, Soho Theatre's Writers' Lab, HighTide Academy, and he is currently one of four young writers on Hampstead Theatre's Inspire: The Next Playwright Programme. James's plays include *Fast Food*, starring Jude Law (Lyric Hammersmith; Lyric Gala 2017), *Ordinary Boys* (Royal Court; Playlist), *Street Life* (Norwich Theatre Royal), *Uniform* (Oldham Coliseum) and *Man Hug* (Theatre Royal BSE; Winner of Anglian Voices Playwriting Competition 2017). James recently developed his new plays *Time and Tide* on Park Theatre's Script Accelerator programme and *Fifty Years* on the Criterion Theatre's New Writing Programme. James is currently under commission to write new plays for HighTide, Eastern Angles and Norwich Arts Centre and he is developing TV projects with Hat Trick, Big Talk and Hare & Tortoise. James has been longlisted for the Bruntwood, Papatango and Verity Bargate playwriting prizes. When James isn't writing, he works as a diversity consultant at Norwich Arts Centre and teaches scriptwriting at Norwich Theatre Royal, New Wolsey Ipswich and Marina Theatre Lowestoft. James is represented by Independent Talent.

AUTHOR'S NOTE

Growing up queer in rural England, I felt like a ghost no one believed in, as I never saw contemporary rural queer life represented onstage, on screen or in print. So I decided to write *Rubber Ring* to help me better understand myself, to help the play's rural queer audiences feel less invisible and to help all audiences of the play better understand and reassess how they perceive rural queer life. *Rubber Ring* has toured the UK on and off for the last two years and I am currently adapting it for TV with Hat Trick Productions. I am amazed and moved by the life the play has had on the stage and I am delighted that the script is being published by Samuel French so that the play can have a permanent life on the page. I hope you enjoy reading this playtext or staging your own production of the play. Thanks for picking it up.

James McDermott, 2019

CHARACTER

This was originally written and performed as a play for one actor.

SCRIPT NOTES

Speech in bold indicates when the performer addresses the audience.

Rubber Ring was first performed with no set and no props.

Rubber Ring was first produced at The Pleasance Islington on the 31 October 2016.

Written and performed by James McDermott

Directed by Siobhan James-Elliott
Produced by Nikolai Ribnikov, Nick Smith and Thomas Jones.

Front cover image by Gareth J. Smith
garethjsmith@outlook.com

ACKNOWLEDGEMENTS

Thanks to Siobhan James-Elliott for directing the first production of this play with such passion, precision and playfulness; thanks to Nikolai Ribnikov, Nick Smith and Thomas Jones for producing the first production of this play and for giving me my first break as a playwright; thanks to Steve Waters for being the warmest, wisest scriptwriting teacher and for mentoring me during the writing of *Rubber Ring*; thanks to Julia Sowerbutts of INK and Patrick Morris of Menagerie Theatre Company for helping me develop early drafts of this script; thanks to Scott Brown for letting Siobhan and me rehearse this play in the UEA Drama Studio; thanks to Karen Jeremiah and everyone at Creative Arts East for helping me tour *Rubber Ring*; thanks to Rob Salmon, China Plate and everyone at New Wolsey's Pulse Festival who awarded *Rubber Ring* Pulse Festival's Suitcase Prize in 2017; thanks to my former agent Micheline Steinberg for supporting me when I was developing 'Rubber Ring'; thanks to my agents Jessi Stewart and Anwar Chentoufi for their endless encouragement, patience and guidance; thanks to Pasco-Q Kevlin and Lucy Farrant at Norwich Arts Centre and Stephen Crocker and Wendy Ellis at Norwich Theatre Royal for all the help and opportunities; thanks to Jo and Matt O'Neill for encouraging me to pursue acting; thanks to Rachel Connor for encouraging me to pursue writing, getting me into reading and helping me to come out and be brave enough to be myself; thanks to Russell T. Davies, Jonathan Harvey and Tom Wells, whose work made me want to write drama, helped me to understand myself and showed terrified teenage me that everything might just be alright; thanks to Mum and Dad for the love, for raising me on old sitcoms and for never telling me to get a safer job; and thanks to Morrissey, whose music has shaped me, saved me and influenced the writing of this play. I am grateful to you all.

*To Mum, Dad, Shiv, Morrissey and anyone who has grown
up queer in a rural community*

1.

I'm gonna tell you a story.

MUM Knock knock, lover.

And it starts at eight thirty when Mum knocks on my bedroom door.

Can I have a word?

JIMMY Have two: piss off.

But in she trots, nearly trips over my pile of choose-your-own-adventure books, then perches on the end of my bed.

MUM Don't swear at me lover, please, thank you. It spoils you. And open a window. It mings in here.

JIMMY It didn't until you came in.

MUM I don't ming. Smell me. That's ylang-ylang. Radox. It mings cos you're never out this room, are ya? Locked in here day and night with your records and your reading. Before you hit sixteen and started listening to that Morrissey, you were never in. Always off gallivanting. Right little Ray Mears, you were. But now... Ya dad's cummerbund has more outings than you. You're reclusive, lover.

JIMMY Of course I'm reclusive. We live in Sheringham. The coastal town they forgot to bomb. This place is a recluse. This place is a prison. And all the other inmates are thatched and pebble-dashed and they stink. Of potatoes. And molluscs. Why couldn't you bring me up in the city where the people are young and smell of money and perfume? Herbs?

MUM Herbs? What d'ya wanna smell of herbs for?

JIMMY   Look. Leave it. I'm fine, alright? Happy as Larry.

MUM   I knew a Larry once. Killed himself. He might not've done if he'd told his mum what was really wrong with him. Look, lover. Me and you, we used to be thick as thieves. So talk to me. What's up?

What's up?

I'm sixteen, I don't know whether I like boys or girls and I live in Sheringham.

I'm fucked.

Well I'm not actually; that's the problem...

Where can I "explore" by the coast?

Rock pools.

I can't get onto Grindr and Tinder; there's no 4G in Norfolk.

The whole world is a singles' bar now but I can't get in.

I am sick of feeling like a story that will never get told.

That's what's up.

Of course I don't say any of that to Mum...

Instead I say:

JIMMY   I'm just sad I can't go and see Morrissey at the O2 tomorrow. I only need fifty quid for a ticket. And another twenty nine quid for travel but... Seven quid Sheringham to Norwich, twenty-quid Norwich to Stratford Underground, two quid Stratford Underground to North Greenwich then a two-minute walk. I know what I'm doing. I've Googled it.

MUM   You are not going to London on your own. Who d'ya think you are: Dick Whittington?

JIMMY No but I think you are. A dick, I mean... Mum. You've just said I'm reclusive. When I say I want to go out, you try and stop me. I can't win.

MUM Look. Here's a tenner. Go and buy one of them books ya love, choose your own adventures. That'll get you out the house. Just get out this bloody bedroom. Promise me?

And I clock the Morrissey poster on my bedroom wall...

And I swear the Mozziah winks at me...

JIMMY I promise...

*

I cycle to school and try to beat the steam train out of town.

But as always, it wins and whistles a laugh as I'm stopped in my tracks by streets upon streets upon streets of chip shops and gift shops and pound shops.

Everywhere I look, I'm passed by lovers entwined.

Giggling groups make their way to Broadmoor.

Or school, as I'm told I should call it.

And no one notices me...

But I don't care.

I don't...

Cos...people in London will notice me.

Yeah.

I'm gonna get that eighty quid.

I'm gonna get that Morrissey ticket.

And I'm gonna get out of this town.

How though?

How am I gonna find another seventy quid in a day?

I stop on the promenade.

The sea and the sky are the same shade of grey, a wall between me and the universe.

And as I look out at the universe, I wonder if that's all I'll ever get to do.

Just look at it...

When is my story gonna start then?

*

As I cycle past the Pearly Gates Retirement Home, I see that someone else's story is coming to an end...

I walk over to see if it's my old neighbour when a hand grabs mine.

It's Brian, bad-breathed Brian, in his Crocs and corduroy slacks.

**Brian is the resident carer but he looks older than
any of the residents.**

JIMMY That isn't Mrs M, is it, Brian? On the stretcher?

BRIAN Norris, it is. On the stretcher. Seventy-four, he was.
Good age.

JIMMY It wasn't for Norris: he died.

BRIAN Sixty-three, my Maureen, when she tripped over that
quiche. I haven't been able to look short crust pastry in
the eye since. Sixty-three's no age, is it? You've gotta get
out and live when ya can, lad. Cos age will creep up on ya.

JIMMY Good: at least old people know who they are... Is Mrs
M in her room?

BRIAN I've sat her in front of *Murder She Wrote*. Here: she
won twenty quid on the tombola yesterday. Yeah. I won a
quiche... Tell her I'll be in with her Maxwell House in a tick.

*

I shout into Mrs M's good ear:

JIMMY Morning Mrs M. How are you keeping?

MRS M Oh duck, I'm knackered. Brian woke me up in the
middle of the night, didn't he? He said he forgot to gimme
my sleeping pills. Well I couldn't get back off after that. I
spent rest of night just staring at that poster they've framed
on my wall, "love laugh live", ya seen it? Any road, shush,
I'm missing *Murder She Wrote*. It's the black one who did
it, I'm tellin' ya.

Mrs M makes Donald Trump sound like Ghandi.

But she used to buy me Capri-Suns, so every cloud.

Mrs M is sat in her overcoat.

Her suitcase is packed by her chair.

As per, she says:

Today's the day. Today's the day my man comes to take me away.

It's as I'm dreaming that anyone would come to take me away that I clock Mrs M's purse...

And the twenty-pound note peeping out of it...

Surely I can't be about to steal from Mrs M?

Go on! Do it!

JIMMY What?

MRS M I'm talking to Jessica Fletcher! Nick the bastard!

And so before you can say Angela Lansbury...

My hand is in Mrs M's purse, the twenty-pound note is in my pocket and I'm out in the corridor.

JIMMY I've gotta run Mrs M. I'm, er, late for school...

I'm a thief.

I'm a common criminal.

I'm...

I'm a protagonist!

I'm in a story!

I'm –.

*

MS SHANKLY Late, McDermott.

JIMMY Are you, Miss? So am I.

MS SHANKLY It's Ms. Get changed. Now.

Belligerent ghouls work in Sheringham schools and they don't come more belligerent than headmistress and games mistress Sylvia Shankly.

JIMMY I, er, can't do PE today, Miss. I'm poorly. Tummy ache.

MS SHANKLY I have tinnitus and a grumbling ovary. Try that for poorly. Changed. Now. Where was I? Joyce? Here. Rourke? Here. McDermott?

CRAIG Queer!

Craig Webster.

A boy that ignorant, if you shot him in the head he'd just whistle.

Craig makes Putin sound like Peter Tatchell but everyone loves him cos he's as "fit as fuck".

Not that I see it myself...

MS SHANKLY Webster. A word. Outside. And what are you doing with all that money? You better not be selling Pritt Sticks again?

CRAIG I'm not, Miss.

MS SHANKLY It's Ms. Boys: outside. And don't run. That bell is a sign for me, not for you. What do you mean "What bell?" Wasn't there one? Bloody tinnitus... Right. Webster: with me! McDermott: changed! Boys: outside!

And an army of rhinos in football boots charge past, stinking of Lynx.

Leaving me alone with Craig's blazer.

With Craig's money…

And so before you can say grumbling ovary, my hand is in Craig's pocket and inside I find…

A pack of backy…

A shit load of Pritt Sticks…

But right at the bottom of his pocket I find…

Fifty quid!

Last warning, Webster. Now get your report card out your blazer.

Shit!

Shankly heads back into the changing room, Craig heads straight for his blazer…

CRAIG You've had my fifty quid.

JIMMY Can I go to the toilet, Miss? It's the tummy ache.

CRAIG I'll give you bollock ache in a minute. Now empty. Your. Pockets.

And Craig's that close I can taste his words.

They taste of Red Bull and roll-ups.

SHANKLY McDermott! Empty your pockets. Or I'll frisk you myself.

I don't fancy being frisked by Shankly: she has nails that'd make Freddie Krueger jealous.

So I have no choice but to turn out my pockets…

CRAIG You thieving little queer.

MS SHANKLY McDermott! My office! Now!

JIMMY But, Miss!

MS SHANKLY IT'S MS!

*

It's like a game of three-way ping pong in Shankly's office.

JIMMY But, Mum, he was calling me stuff.

MS SHANKLY That's not the issue here, Mrs McDermott.

MUM I'll decide what the issue is, Miss Jean Brodie. Now forget the thieving lark, what's Craig called my boy?

MS SHANKLY He called your son queer.

Silence.

And the silence grows louder and louder as that word gets bigger and bigger and hangs in the air between us.

If this were the Sahara and not Sheringham, a tumbleweed would roll across the floor...

Mrs McDermott. The school can offer your boy a wide variety of leaflets and or...condoms, ugh, if he's having problems with his sexuality.

MUM He's not. Are you, lover?

JIMMY No... I don't know... And I only stole money from Craig and Mrs M so I could afford to get out and find out. Here's Mrs M's twenty. Do you want back the tenner you gave me?

And I can't tell whether Mum's blinking away tears...

Or whether she winks at me...

Winks at me and gives me a look that says:

Run. Get out. Choose adventure.

And so I bullet out that office and I run down the corridor and boys girls everyone is noticing me and I'm outside I'm at the bike sheds and I cycle out of Broadmoor past the chip shops and gift shops and pound shops past the thatched pebble-dashed people and suddenly I'm at the station and the train to Norwich is just about to leave…

Excuse me: phone.

"Craig Webster posted on your wall."

Facebook – delete app?

Delete.

"Mum – call incoming."

Block contact?

Sorry, Mum.

Right: I have a tenner, thirty-six per cent phone battery and a day to get my hands on a Morrissey ticket.

Do I choose adventure?

2.

TANNOY This is the eleven forty-four service from Sheringham to Norwich calling at you chose to board the train, you're finally getting out of Sheringham and you are gonna get laid in London due to arrive into Norwich at twelve forty-four.

I've locked myself in the lavs to avoid the fare. Textbook.

But as the train's wheels start turning, my mind starts churning...

No money no ticket no friends.

No money no ticket no friends.

No money no ticket no friends.

No money no ticket –.

No.

I can't go back.

Go back and I'll be expelled.

I'm in exile.

Like Wilde.

Oh my God, I'm Morrissey!

He fled his humdrum town and moved to the city.

At twenty-three...

With a record deal...

I can't sing.

I can't do anything.

I mean, I'm alright with a diablo but...

Shuddup.

I'm Morrissey.

I'm actually Morrissey.

But Morrissey went to London with The Smiths...

Who do I have?

Who will I stay with?

*

Before I know it I'm at Norwich station and me and my bike are being carried along the platform by a sea of suits and shoes and coffee cups towards the:

TANNOY   Twelve forty-seven to Liverpool Street calling at no money no ticket no friends due to arrive into London at fourteen thirty-four.

Do I choose to board the train?

Or do I pussy out, get back in the bogs and head home to Sheringham?

*

JIMMY Sorry this is the train to Liverpool Street, right? Hello?
Rude.

I get onto a carriage with a cycle rack – yes – but no
toilet – shit – nowhere to hide...

There must be one further along the train.

But then I'm knocked into a seat by an arse that's
big enough to show films on.

And I'm just about to get up to find a lav to hide in
when she sits at my table.

And I decide to stay exactly where I am...

*

She's reading one of those celebrity magazines.

You...

Closer...

Heat...

Now...

OK...

I can't see which one.

I wonder if she smells of herbs...

Then she clocks me staring at her.

And she smiles at me with her eyes...

Come on, Mcdermott.

Say something to her.

Say anything to her...

Shit: she's looking back at her magazine.

How do you start a conversation with a stranger?

Conversation is so much easier on...

Tinder!

If she's on Tinder I can find out her name.

"Loading, loading..."

I can start a conversation.

"Finding people in your area..."

Claire.

No.

Tracey.

No.

Beth.

Hell no!

Bonnie.

Bonnie Marr, nineteen...

That's her!

Bonnie...

Wee Bonnie lass.

She could be Scottish?

No: she doesn't look drunk.

Bonnie Langford?

Bonnie Langford could be her mum?

Or...

Bonnie Tyler!

Bonnie Tyler could be her mum?

Bonnie Tyler would know Morrissey, course she would, Bonnie Tyler could get me tickets for tomorrow night's Morrissey concert...

Swipe right?

It's a match.

Yes!

Ping.

No!

Don't check your phone, Bonnie!

She's gonna see that it's me who matched with her.

She's gonna want a conversation.

What am I gonna say to her?

Oh my God this is terrible...

Bonnie looks at her phone, then she looks at me...

And I feel my cheeks turn a colour that hurts.

Then she smiles at me with her mouth as well as her eyes.

BONNIE Hi kiss.

She messaged me...

She actually messaged me...

JIMMY Hallo kiss.

Hallo?

I'm supposed to be Casanova not Enid Blyton...

BONNIE Hallo 2 U 2! Ur fit kiss.

I'm fit!

And I got another kiss!

This isn't terrible.

This is terri-brill.

JIMMY Ur fat 2 kiss.

Shit!

Sorry. Typo. I meant ur fit not fat. Kiss...

And Bonnie's smile grows wider like a door opening...

Phew!

BONNIE Where u gettin off kiss?

JIMMY Stratford Underground. U?

BONNIE Colchester. Mine's the next stop. Maybe we could... get off together winky face?

Word play.

Sexy suggestive word play.

And a winky face...

Say yes?

Say no: I need to get to London.

I need to get a Morrissey ticket.

Moz. Comes. First.

Well?

Just say something to her.

Say anything to her...

INSPECTOR Tickets please. Thanking you, Miss. Tickets, Sir.

JIMMY Em... A single to... Stratford Underground please.

And Bonnie's smile falls into a frown faster than a door slamming shut...

INSPECTOR That'll be seventeen poundingtons please.

JIMMY What?! Em... Mum's paying. Yeah... But she's...in the lavs. With her handbag. She'll be ages. She's...on her period. And she has the shits...

The inspector's mouth hangs open, the train doors slide open...

And Bonnie's gone...

Sorry this is my stop.

INSPECTOR Right well do you have a valid ticket to Colchester?

*

But the inspector becomes white noise because me and my bike are on the platform and we're being carried along by a sea of suits and shoes and coffee cups.

Where is she?

I look left...

Right...

Left again...

But she's gone.

She's gone...

And I'm in Colchester...

Is Colchester London?

TANNOY The next train to Stratford leaves in twenty minutes. The next train to Norwich leaves in three minutes.

No.

I'm not going home.

I chose adventure.

I'm going to see Morrissey.

Shit: are concert tickets still available?

"Loading web page..."

"Unable to load ticketmaster.com"

What?!

I thought it was only in Norfolk that you can't get 4G...

I can't get onto Google to find out if Morrissey tickets are still available.

I can't get onto Google Maps to find out if Colchester is in London.

JIMMY Em, excuse me...sorry could you tell me if...hello sorry is Colchester in...

London people weren't supposed to find me invisible...

Right, what do I do?

Do I go on the thief, try and nick enough money for the train fare to Stratford?

Do I get on my bike and...cycle to London?

Or do I do the sensible thing and just get the train back home?

*

"London – sixty-six miles."

You have to be kidding me?

I've been cycling up this hillside for yonks.

The air is heavy and smoky and hot.

I wish it was light and salty and cold...

No I don't.

I chose adventure.

I'm in a story.

This is just...a shit chapter, that's all.

Yeah.

Yeah I'm off to London.

But which part of London?

Which part of London is sixty-six –.

PPPFFFFFFFFFFFFFFFFFFFFFFFFF!

What the?

My bike smashes to a stand-still, my head whiplashes forward as on a desolate hillside...

A puncture.

But then...

A charming car pulls up beside me and in the driver's seat I see...

Bonnie!

BONNIE Hallo. Fancy a ride?

*

BONNIE You...pulled away Jimmy? This, is what you want isn't it?

JIMMY Yeahyeahyeah no course it is just...no just as soon as I got in the car, you pulled into this underpass and started to...y'know? Maybe we could...talk, for a bit, first?

Em... Tell me a bit about yourself. Tell me about London.

BONNIE I'm horny, London's expensive and I have work in ten minutes. Come here.

You...flinched Jimmy?

JIMMY Sorry just...the gear stick's kinda getting in the way. And ooh look: I'm sat on your purse... Sorry. Your hand just...took me by surprise a bit, that's all.

BONNIE If you wanna take me by surprise at all then feel free. To feel me.

JIMMY Right. Right... Em. Cool. Cool...

BONNIE Ow! Slapping me on the breasts for?! You have hands like gammon. This isn't really working, is it? What is it, what's wrong? Are you a virgin?

JIMMY No. I've had sex with loads of women. Loads. Seen more tits than... Bill Oddie.

BONNIE Then what's wrong with me?

JIMMY Nothing's wrong with you, you're lovely.

BONNIE Then what's wrong with you? Come on, what is it? Just be straight with me. Oh... Wait. You saying you're—

JIMMY No. I don't know... Look, I'm sorry, I thought I'd be able to go through with this. When I've watched, films and that – *Seven Brides for Seven Brides*, *Womb Raider* – they've done nothing for me but. I thought I'd be able to do something for real with a woman. Morrissey has. He's had loads.

BONNIE Like you, ya mean? I might just be the wrong girl.

JIMMY I can tell in my bones that this doesn't fit.

BONNIE And you think boys will fit?

JIMMY Well they must do if girls don't, right? And that's...okay. Cos, yeah, Morrissey's had loads of boys too so. Your face: you must know who Morrissey is?

BONNIE I know I have to be at work in five minutes...

JIMMY Yeah. Sorry... I mean what I said: your eyes are lovely.

BONNIE I mean what I said too: your hands are like gammon.

*

Bonnie drops me off at a crossroads in... Great Dunmow?!

I wave her off with one hand, clutch the thirty quid I nicked from her purse in the other.

Kerching!

I only need another tenner then I have enough for a Morrissey ticket!

But...how much is a room for the night gonna cost me?

And a new bike: Bonnie's just driven off with mine in her boot...

Excuse me: phone.

Grindr: "1 new message from... Cockcraver1988".

Call your son that and he's bound to be gay...

MIKE Toned, uncut n I samba every Saturday. Up 4 fun? Can offer accom kiss.

"Accom"?

Accommodation!

Free accommodation!

Course he'll only offer accommodation after I've...

Let's hope I can get "up 4 fun"...

MIKE I'm four hundred feet away in Dick Van Dyke's gay bar. Meet me?

Say no?

I can't go clubbing: I don't have a stitch to wear.

Say yes?

Free accommodation...

My first gay bar...

JIMMY "C U there."

This is it...

This is London!

I've arrived!

*

This is not like the bars described in Wilde's letters or Isherwood's diaries...

No one is smoking Sobranie Black Russians or reading the works of Camus...

Everyone is reading their iPhones.

And the clientele aren't boys so much as...

Men.

Men who all look up from their phones...

And look through me.

And in this moment I have never felt more alone in my life.

In this moment I want to be anyone else anywhere else in any other story in the world.

And I'm just about to leave when my eyes find...

His?

Hers?

I can't tell under the lights.

But they are the only one in the club who's dancing.

Her Adam's apple is bigger than a boxing glove...

His blouse blows about her vest...

Her package bulges out of his leather trousers...

He is the most beautiful girl I've ever seen.

No...

She is the most handsome boy I've ever seen.

Then a big beefy hand slaps me on the shoulder...

MIKE Jimmy? Uncut? Six inches?

JIMMY Either these are very tight jeans or you've read my Grindr profile. Cockcraver1988?

MIKE My friends call me Mike. Or Pudsey Bear. You, er, ready to shoot off to mine?

JIMMY Em... I've just paid eight quid to get in so—

MIKE It's dead in here. And listen: I have history with the barman, don't I? No, don't fucking look at him. I stormed out of his last week, didn't I? Dirty bastard asked if he could piss in my mouth. I said "Listen, you fucking nonce", I said. "There's shitloads of glucose in urine. I'm diabetic." So: you coming back to mine or what?

*

MIKE You...pulled away? My breath, innit? It's that kebab. Look, there's Smints in my bedside cabinet if it's rank?

JIMMY Your breath's fine.

MIKE Is it the kissing then cos the fella I was with this morning said I kiss like a bulldog eating porridge?

JIMMY What, no, the kissing's fine too.

MIKE What did you pull away for then? You aren't a virgin, are ya?

JIMMY No. I've had sex with loads of men. Loads... Just, a little uncomfy, that's all.

MIKE Cos you're sat on my wallet look... You'd be more comfy out of that T shirt. I'll take mine off too look.

JIMMY You're very hairy...

MIKE Pudsey Bear, mate, Pudsey Bear. You top or bottom? It didn't say on your profile.

JIMMY I dunno...

MIKE You're versatile? Right! You wanna top or bottom me then?

JIMMY Em... I'll, go on top.

MIKE You'll bottom me?

JIMMY What? No, I'll top you, I'll go on top.

MIKE Nah. You top me, you fuck me. But there's no chance of that happening with that thing. Look at ya. That was like a baby's arm a minute ago. Now it's like a baby's penis... It's the kissing that made you lose it, wasn't it? I knew I shouldn't have had that kebab.

JIMMY It isn't because of your breath.

MIKE Then what is it? Cos I dancercise. I samba every Saturday. I'm in great nick, mate.

JIMMY No I know you are, look at you, it's just... I had a lot to drink at Dick Van Dyke's.

MIKE Bollocks did ya: you had a Hooch.

JIMMY Can you pass me my T shirt please?

MIKE What?

JIMMY Can you pass me my T shirt please?

MIKE Oh for f – you're lucky I'm a nice guy. I'm not a lab rat for little kids to experiment on.

JIMMY Yeah I've come to London on my own so I'm not a kid, alright? It's just... Look at you. The muscle, the hair... You're such...a man.

MIKE Pudsey Bear, mate. Pudsey Bear.

JIMMY I'm sorry. I thought I'd be able to go through with this. When I've watched, films and that – *Schindler's Fist, Buttman and Throbbin'* – they've done nothing for me but. I thought I'd be able to do something for real with a man. Morrissey's had loads. Your face: you must know who Morrissey is?

MIKE I've never heard of her. Look: do you want a drink or something before you go?

JIMMY Go? You offered accommodation.

MIKE Yeah and you offered fun.

JIMMY Fun doesn't just have to be sex.

MIKE You got a Ludo set in your back pocket, have ya? I'll sort ya that drink.

Shit.

No accommodation...

Then I spot his wallet.

And the three twenty-pound notes sticking out of it...

No.

It's too risky.

He's a bear.

He'd kill me.

He's Pudsey Bear: he's supposed to help Children in Need.

I'll just pocket two...

Got em.

Ooh shit here he comes.

I only have Hooch. Is that alright?

JIMMY Thanks. You not having one?

MIKE Full of sugar, mate. I'm not risking it. And look: you can kip on my floor if ya desperate.

Come on then. Where are you from, Dick Whittington?

JIMMY Bored and lazed in Sheringham.

MIKE Yeah? My granddad just died there.

JIMMY That's all there is to do there.

MIKE Tell me about it. Skeggy was just as bad. Soon as I could, fifty quid out my dad's wallet, Megabus to Victoria, goodnight Vienna. I wanted life, lights, noise, boys. Regular buses. I was gonna become a millionaire. I became a sales assistant. Nando's. There's a Nando's in Skeggy. Cos I fucked my time away at school, didn't I? When I was your age, I handled more meat than Bernard Matthews. Now I'm handling it for a job. Chicken I mean, at Nando's, not cock. I'm not a rent boy. Hang on: phone. Bloody hell: that barman wants to come over and let me piss in his mouth. Yeah sorry, mate, you're gonna have to go.

JIMMY Go? You've just said I can kip on your floor. Can't you go to his?

MIKE We can't do anything at his cos of the greyhound.

JIMMY Well can't I come back when you've finished? I haven't finished my Hooch.

MIKE Take it with ya.

JIMMY Take it where?

MIKE I dunno. Sheringham?

JIMMY Thanks. You're right. I am lucky you're such a nice guy. I'm lucky everyone is round here...

*

11pm and I am standing in the doorway of Dick Van Dyke's.

This is not the story I wanted to be in.

London people were supposed to give a shit.

And I was supposed to get laid.

I can't even get it up.

Morrissey could get it up.

Or...could he?

Is that why he was celibate?

Oh my God: am I celibate?

Me and Moz are so alike!

At least I have enough money for a Morrissey ticket.

"Loading webpage..."

"Tickets for this event are sold out".

Refresh.

"Tickets for this event are sold out".

Refresh.

"Tickets for this event are" –.

No.

Outta battery.

You have to be kidding me?!

THUG Empty your pockets, you tranny.

What the...?

At the bus stop, a mugger has...that boy, that girl, that person from the club by the throat.

Shit a brick...

Do I phone the police?

I can't: I don't have any battery...

Do I...run over and...intervene?

I can't: I don't have any balls...

But then...

Then I hear those words...

THUG Empty your pockets. You *queer*.

*

JIMMY Oi! Leave him...her...alone or...I'll call the police.

THUG For a fucking tranny?

BILLY I am more of a man than you are and more of a woman than you'll ever get but I am not a tranny, alright?

JIMMY Look. If I give you...seventy quid...will you just go?

And that's it.

No money.

No ticket.

Friends?

BILLY What were you doing? I could've handled that.

JIMMY I've just lost seventy quid for you!

BILLY Don't expect me to pay you back.

JIMMY I don't expect anything from people round here.

BILLY I'm not some damsel in distress who needs rescuing, alright?

JIMMY Cos you're more of a man than I am and more of a woman than I'll ever get?

See ya.

BILLY Wait where ya going? The bus is here in a minute. Wait! Thanks. For stopping. For losing your money for me.

JIMMY That's alright. I guess I'm just a gentleman, aren't I?

BILLY Ooh I hope not. I'm Billy.

JIMMY Jimmy. Your lip, it's bleeding.

BILLY It'll heal. It usually does. Nice Morrissey T shirt. What's your favourite song?

JIMMY "Rubber Ring". Yours?

BILLY "Let Me Kiss You".

JIMMY What?

BILLY Off 2004's *You Are the Quarry*?

JIMMY Oh yeah. Good song...

BILLY Look, Jimmy. What are you doing tomorrow night? Cos my sister's just been involved in a hit and run accident and – oh no don't worry, she's alright, she was the driver, dozy mare, looking at ten years bless her – but she was supposed to be coming down to see Moz with me so—

JIMMY Moz? As in Morrissey? At the O2?

BILLY There's a ticket going spare if you fancy it? Consider it thanks.

JIMMY Oh my God! If only you knew what I've been through trying to get a ticket. Shall I, em, call you tomorrow to collect the ticket or – shit I can't: I'm outta battery.

BILLY Why don't you...come round tonight? To, em...collect the ticket? And...charge your battery? You...pulled away Jimmy?

JIMMY What are you?

BILLY Here's me thinking you were different. Here's the bus. See ya.

JIMMY I wasn't talking to you. I don't know what I am.

BILLY I'm Billy. That's who I am. You're Jimmy. Our names are the only labels that matter, darling, now are you coming back to mine or what?

Morrissey slept with boys...

Morrissey slept with girls...

Morrissey never slept with boys who might be girls, girls who might be boys...

*

JIMMY Nice room.

BILLY Ah thanks. Just student digs, nothing special. Look I er,
     probably won't be able to kiss or er, suck, anything, tonight,
     cos of my lip but. We could just...talk? You could tell me
     about yourself? I could tell you about London?

JIMMY Yeah that sounds nice.

And so we talk time away.

**Billy has some chocolate body paint but as we don't
wanna use it we have it on toast, we have it in bed
and we listen to our favourite Smiths songs.**

This Charming Man

This Night Has Opened My Eyes

Asleep

But when I fall asleep...

I hear the sound of the sea...

*

We wake at midday!

**Billy doesn't have any make-up on and so she looks
more like a boy.**

I tell her that's okay.

**Billy puts his make-up on and so he looks more like
a girl.**

I tell him that's okay too.

We decide to spend the day in London.

We hide in the train toilets on the way in to avoid the fare. Textbook.

Billy takes me to Tower Bridge.

But the sky and the Thames are the same shade of grey...

Billy buys me a pink gin in a Soho bar called Tequila Mockingbird.

But the staff treat me as if I'm invisible and the place smells of...

Molluscs...

Billy tells me about the council estate she grew up on.

I tell him about the seaside town I grew up in.

Billy tells me about his Dad who used to hit her and his mum who used to be alive.

I tell her about Dad, who's a fisherman, and Mum...

Who calls me lover...

Then Billy tells me it's five o'clock so we should probably be heading to the O2.

Then Billy hands me my Morrissey ticket.

And then I see the sign first:

"Due to artist's illness this evening's concert has been cancelled..."

JIMMY All this way. All this. And for what?

BILLY Ooh thanks. My lip feels better now. Well it doesn't but... I'm not waiting any longer for you to kiss me.

And in that moment I realise that I'm in the best kind of story.

A love story.

And I pray that this is the end of it.

Please please please let –.

MUM Lover? Oh, lover, thank God you're safe, come here, hold me.

JIMMY Mum? What are you doing here?

MUM I prayed you'd be here. I shot down in your dad's Daewoo Matiz. I'm sure I got a ticket going through Colchester.

JIMMY Mum... I'm not coming home. I'm staying here with Billy.

MUM Listen, Julian Clary: he's not staying here with you.

BILLY I know he isn't. Cos I've known you a day, darling. And today's been amazing. I'll tell stories about today. But this story has to come to an end. Or this chapter of it, at least.

JIMMY No. I don't belong among people who are happy living life from their living rooms.

MUM No one's spent much time in their living rooms this past day, lover. Every one's been out looking for you. You are talk of the town. Right little celebrity. Like Morrissey.

JIMMY Am I?! No... No. That humdrum town corrodes my soul.

BILLY No it doesn't. Morrissey might slag off seaside towns but all you've done since I met you is rave about yours. Don't listen to Morrissey. Morrissey stood you up. Morrissey doesn't care about you. Your mum does. Your town does. So, darling: what do you do?

3.

JIMMY Mum, stop the car. Turn around, I've changed my mind, I'm not going back to Broadmoor.

MUM You won't have any more trouble from that Miss Shankly.

JIMMY It's Ms.

MUM And she thought tinnitus could give her ear ache...

JIMMY Craig's bullying is only gonna get worse now I stole from him. This isn't the end of an adventure story. This is the beginning of a horror story.

MUM Oh look, there's an ambulance outside the Pearly Gates. Oh my God, that's Mrs M...

JIMMY What? Stop the car, Mum. Mum. Stop the car.

*

BRIAN She was watching *Bergerac*. She got up to go to the lav when she tripped over that suitcase she leaves packed by her chair. She banged her head on the wall and that framed "love laugh life" poster came crashing down, smacked her on the bonce.

JIMMY But she's alright, Brian, isn't she, she's breathing, she's going to be okay?

BRIAN Seventy-nine she was. Good age. Sixty three, my Maureen, when she tripped over that quiche. "Love laugh live". What a load of old... No. No you've got to, haven't ya? Whoever, wherever you are. Cos you never know when the Grim Reaper will come knocking. Anyway. Funeral to look forward to. Sorry I don't know why I said that... Em... I'll do you both a Maxwell House.

And Brian goes, leaving me alone with Mum.

MUM Whoever you are lover... I love the bones of you, you
know that, don't ya?

JIMMY I love the bones of you too.

And as a tear snakes down onto my lip...

I swear it tastes of Capri-Sun...

*

I'm walking home when on the beach I spot:

CRAIG Queer! I heard you pissed off to London to find Mozza?

JIMMY Not just to find him. What are you doing on the beach,
Craig?

CRAIG Just sniffing a bit of Pritt Stick. What are you doing
back in this shit hole?

JIMMY It's not that bad.

CRAIG Neither are you, I suppose: cos of all the ear ache your
mum gave her, Shankly's taking some time off work. Wanna
sniff of this Pritt Stick? There's a tinny going here too if ya
fancy it? What ya waiting for?

JIMMY A punchline. A punch. And Mozza? Only his fans call
him Mozza.

CRAIG Fucking love Morrissey, me. The Smiths. Quality.

JIMMY What's your favourite song?

CRAIG "Sweet and Tender Hooligan". Yours?

JIMMY "Let Me Kiss You".

CRAIG What?

JIMMY Off... 2004's *You Are the Quarry*?

CRAIG Oh yeah. Good song...

JIMMY Listen, Craig... When Morrissey reschedules that London concert...do you wanna...

CRAIG Yeah. Maybe. Don't go telling everyone though. I'm not queer.

JIMMY Me neither. I'm Jimmy. You're Craig. Our names are the only labels that matter. Right?

CRAIG What the fuck are you talking about?

*

MUM Knock knock, lover. Can I have a word?

JIMMY Have two, Mum: piss off. I'm trying to get ready to go out.

MUM You've been out every night this week since you got back from London. Where are you off tonight?

JIMMY Just a friend's. From school. Why all the questions, Juliet Bravo?

MUM No reason. You just used to be so reclusive that's all. Locked in here day and night with your records and your reading. Don't give up on ya books, lover. Take ya far, will them.

JIMMY Yeah well, I'm not sure I wanna go far.

MUM You're gonna escape, see the world.

JIMMY I've only just started to see Sheringham. There's the rest of Norfolk to see first.

MUM You can't stay round here. What are ya gonna do with yourself round here?

JIMMY I dunno. Get a job, get some mates, fall in love, do what everybody else does. Same old story. But it might be an adventure.

MUM Lover. This is a great place to grow up, it's a great place to end up. But the bit in the middle, life, no: that doesn't happen round here. Coffee mornings, Morris dancing: that happens round here.

JIMMY Mum. I'm happy here. Happy as Larry.

MUM Until Larry's had his fun. Explored, got bored, decided he'd be happier with someone else. And listen... The Larry I knew. Who...died... He was like you. He hated it round here. Then he met someone, decided to settle down. But folk round here... Folk round here didn't like who he'd settled down with. Folk give a man a medal for killing a man. They drive a man to kill himself for loving one. Things have changed in Norfolk, course they have. Just don't end up smelling of molluscs. Get out. Get on. Be someone. Meet someone. Promise me?

JIMMY I promise. What's that smell?

MUM Eh? Oh: jojoba. Nivea.

JIMMY I thought you only ever used Radox?

MUM People change, lover. I mean it: this isn't the end of your story. It's just the end of your first chapter, that's all. Your story is only just beginning.

And that's how my story ends.

VISIT THE SAMUEL FRENCH BOOKSHOP AT THE ROYAL COURT THEATRE

Browse plays and theatre books, get expert advice and enjoy a coffee

Samuel French Bookshop
Royal Court Theatre
Sloane Square
London
SW1W 8AS
020 7565 5024

Shop from thousands of titles on our website

 samuelfrench.co.uk

 samuelfrenchltd

 samuel french uk

9 780573 116322